HARRY POTTER

G·U·I·D·E B·O·O·K

S E R I E S

Book 1 - The Philosopher's Stone
(Also Published as The Sorcerer's Stone)

BOOK 1 SYNOPSIS

Book 1 follows the exploits of a boy named Harry Potter. Harry is the orphaned son of two powerful wizards, James and Lily Potter, who are killed by the dreaded evil wizard Voldemort when Harry is just a year old. Voldemort (also known as He-Who-Must-Not-Be-Named or You-Know-Who) tries to kill Harry as well, and although he does not succeed, the attempt leaves Harry with a lightening-bolt-shaped scar on his forehead.

After his parents' untimely death, Harry is brought to Number Four, Privet Drive to live with his only relatives, Petunia and Vernon Dursley and their young son Dudley. The Dursleys are muggles (non-magic folk) who despise wizards and magic. They are less than pleased that Harry is staying with them, and they keep his magical lineage a secret. Harry is told that his odd scar is the result of a car accident that killed his parents.

The Dursleys are not very nice to Harry, but they dote on their son Dudley. Dudley is a porky, spoiled bully who delights in making Harry's life miserable. One of his favourite pastimes is "Harry hunting" with his big, stupid friends. Harry's round glasses are held together with tape because Dudley has punched him in the nose so often. Dudley has so many toys that he needs an extra bedroom to keep them all in; poor Harry's "bedroom" is a dark

4

dusty, spider-infested "cupboard under the stairs." Dudley gets dozens of presents for his birthday, but Harry never gets anything. Harry has to wear Dudley's hand-me-downs, even though they are far too big for his skinny frame. And when the family goes out, he is usually packed off to stay with mad old Mrs. Figg in her cat-filled, cabbage-smelling house.

Harry first discovers that he is a wizard the summer he turns eleven, when mysterious letters begin to arrive for him. Uncle Vernon panics and takes desperate measures to try to keep the letters away from Harry. He even takes Harry and his family and flees to a ramshackle hut on an isolated rock in the sea, but there is no escape. Just before midnight on the day of his eleventh birthday, Harry finally gets his letter. It is an invitation to attend Hogwarts School of Witchcraft and Wizardry—hand-delivered by the enormous Hagrid, who also brings Harry a large, sticky, somewhat-sat-on chocolate birthday cake. Hagrid tells Harry the truth about his parents' death and explains the mystery of his scar and the miracle of his escape.

In the morning, Harry and Hagrid take a magical boat to London's fabulous Diagon Alley to shop for the supplies Harry will need at his new school. Their first stop is the goblin-guarded wizards' bank, Gringotts, where Hagrid

takes care of some Hogwarts business and Harry withdraw a bit of the fortune that has been left to him by his parents. Then Harry and Hagrid tour the shops of Diagon Alley for wizard's robes, a cloak, a pointed cap, a cauldron, text books, a wand, and other items Harry will need a Hogwarts. At Eeylops Owl Emporium, Hagrid buys Harry his first real birthday present—a snowy-white female owl that Harry names Hedwig.

Hagrid leaves Harry with his train ticket to school on the Hogwarts Express, which leaves from platform nine and three-quarters at London's King's Cross station on September 1 at 11:00 a.m. Harry persuades his Uncle Vernon to take him to the station, where the kindly Mrs. Molly Weasley explains how to get to the scarlet steam engine that will take him to school. On the train, Harry makes the acquaintance of fellow first-years Ron Weasley and Hermione Granger, who are soon to become his best friends. He also meets Neville Longbottom and Ron's twin brothers, as well as the bully Draco Malfoy and his sidekicks Crabbe and Goyle.

Once at Hogwarts, the train is met by Hagrid, who navigates the first-years across a black lake to Hogwarts castle—a magical place where ghosts float about and the people in the portraits go off to visit one another. The sorting

hat sorts first-year students into one of Hogwarts' four houses, named Slytherin, Hufflepuff, Ravenclaw and Gryffindor after the school's four founders. Harry, Ron, Hermione and Neville are delighted to find that they are all assigned to Gryffindor. After a wonderful banquet, Headmaster Dumbledore, whom many consider the greatest wizard ever, cautions that the Forbidden Forest on the school grounds and the right side of the third-floor corridor are out of bounds to students.

Harry later learns that something important is hidden at Hogwarts, guarded by a fierce, three-headed dog whose name is Fluffy. In the meantime, his classes keep him more than busy. He has Charms with Professor Flitwick; Potions with Severus Snape, who doesn't seem to like him; Transfiguration with Professor McGonagall, who can change her desk into a pig; Defence Against the Dark Arts with the stuttering, turbaned Professor Quirrell; History of Magic with the windy old ghost, Professor Binn; and Herbology with Professor Sprout.

Madam Hooch teaches broom-flying. Harry's natural aptitude for this wizardly skill is so impressive that he is invited to join Gryffindor's quidditch team. Quidditch is a fast-paced and sometimes dangerous sport that is a bit like six-hoop basketball played high up in the air. Harry

is the youngest player Hogwarts has seen in a century and the rules are bent to get him his own flying-broom Gryffindor wins the first match of the season against Slytherin, even though Harry's broom acts up. Harry and his friends are convinced that Professor Snape is behind this, and their suspicions are reinforced when Harry follows Snape to a secret rendezvous in the Forbidden Forest.

Christmas at Hogwarts is Harry's best ever. He gets a wooden flute from Hagrid, fudge and a hand-knitted sweater from Ron's mom, a boxful of Chocolate Frogs from Hermione, and even fifty pence from the Dursleys. Best of all, he gets a magical invisibility cloak that belonged to his father, with an anonymous note advising him to use it well. Harry's explorations in his new cloak take him to an out-of-the-way classroom, where he finds the enchanted mirror of erised.

Harry doesn't know it yet, but the mirror will play a part in a great adventure and the quest for the philosopher's stone. In the meantime, like most school children, Harry and his friends get into their share of trouble. Of course, this is usually "magical" trouble—with trolls and dragons and centaurs and unicorns playing a part. But the friends also deal with bigger kinds of trouble, and Harry once again comes face to face with the dark lord Voldemort!

Who's Who And What's What

(All definitions are based on the characters and references
in J.K. Rowling's original Harry Potter books.)

Abbott, Hannah A rosy-cheeked girl with blonde pigtail who starts school at Hogwarts the same year Harr does. Hannah is assigned to Hufflepuff House.

Aconite *See* **Wolfsbane**.

Alchemy An ancient science that deals with making th legendary philosopher's stone.

Alohomora The magic word used to open locked window and doors.

Anti-cheating Spell A spell use to prevent cheating Hogwarts students are required to use quills bewitche with this spell when they write their exams.

Apothecary A bad-smelling but fascinating Diagon Alle shop which sells potion ingredients.

Asphodel A plant whose powdered root is added to a infusion of wormwood to make a sleeping potion s powerful it is known as the draught of living death.

Bagshot, Bathilda Author of *A History of Magic*, one c the required texts for Hogwarts first-years.

ane A black-haired, black-bodied centaur who lives in the Forbidden Forest.

eater A quidditch position. A quidditch team has two beaters who protect their teammates from rocketing bludger balls. The beaters use a small club—like a baseball bat or a rounders bat—to knock the bludgers toward the opposing team. The Weasley twins, Fred and George, are the beaters for the Gryffindor team.

eginners' Guide to Transfiguration, A Written by Emeric Switch. One of the required texts for Hogwarts first-years.

ell, Katie One of the chasers on Gryffindor's quidditch team.

ertie Bott's Every Flavour Beans Candy beans that come in ordinary flavours like chocolate, peppermint and marmalade, and unusual flavours like spinach, liver, tripe, sprouts, toast, coconut, baked bean, strawberry, curry, grass, coffee, sardine, pepper, earwax, and even vomit and bogey.

ezoar A stone taken from the stomach of a goat. It protects against most poisons.

Binns, Professor   A ghost who teaches Harry's boring History of Magic class at Hogwarts.

Black, Sirius   Owner of the large, flying motorcycle which Hagrid borrows to deliver the one-year-old Harry Potter to the Dursley house on Privet Drive.

Bletchley   The keeper on Slytherin's quidditch team.

Bloody Baron   A horrible, staring-eyed, gaunt-faced ghost whose robes are stained with silver blood. The Baron is Slytherin's resident ghost. He is the only one who can control the poltergeist Peeves.

Bludger   One of the three types of balls used in quidditch. Bludger balls are jet black and slightly smaller than the red, soccer-ball-sized quaffle. Two bludger balls are required for a quidditch game. The bludgers are self-propelled and rocket around trying to get past the beaters to knock players off their brooms. They have never killed anyone at Hogwarts, although casualties have included several broken jaws.

Bones, Susan   A first-year student who is assigned to Hufflepuff.

oot, Terry A first-year student who is assigned to Ravenclaw.

rocklehurst, Mandy A first-year student who is assigned to Ravenclaw.

rown, Lavender A first-year student who is assigned to Gryffindor. Lavender is a good friend of Parvinder Patil.

ulstrode, Millicent A first-year student who is assigned to Slytherin.

auldron Cake A type of wizard candy.

entaur A magical creature with the head, arms and upper body of a man and the legs and body of a horse. Centaurs live in the Forbidden Forest. They are deep creatures who read the movements of the planets and foretell the future. They are sworn not to set themselves against the heavens.

haser A quidditch position. A quidditch team has three chasers who score goals by getting the red quaffle ball through one of the three, fifty-foot-high golden

hoops located at each end of the quidditch field. Each goal earns ten points. Angelina Johnson, Katie Bell and Alicia Spinnet are the chasers for the Gryffindor team.

Chocolate Frog A chocolate treat which comes with a trading card that shows famous witches and wizards including Dumbledore, Circe, Cliodna (a druidess), Flamel (an alchemist), Alberic Grunnion, Hengist of Woodcroft, Merlin, Morgana, Paracelsus and others. As in all wizard pictures, the subjects can move around and sometimes even leave for a time.

Cleansweep Seven An above-average flying-broom, but not quite as good as the Nimbus models.

Coat of Arms, Hogwarts The school coat of arms bears the symbols of the four Hogwarts houses—an eagle (for Ravenclaw), a snake (for Slytherin), a lion (for Gryffindor), and a badger (for Hufflepuff)—surrounding a large letter H.

Comet Two Sixty An average flying-broom.

Common Welsh Green A wild dragon native to Britain.

rabbe, Vincent A first-year student who is assigned to Slytherin. Crabbe is one of Draco Malfoy's muscular, thickset, mean-looking, brutish friends. He has a very thick neck and his hair looks like it was cut around a bowl. Crabbe is somewhat taller than his friend Goyle, Malfoy's other sidekick.

rockford, Doris A pipe-smoking old witch who meets Harry at the Leaky Cauldron and keeps coming back to shake his hand.

upboard Under the Stairs This is Harry's room for the first ten years that he lives in the Dursley house on Privet Drive. It is small, dark, and infested with spiders. Harry finally gets his own room the summer he turns eleven, when the Dursleys realize that "somebody" magically knows about the cupboard under the stairs.

urses and Counter-Curses Professor Vindictus Viridian's tip-filled book on bewitching friends and befuddling enemies.

aily Prophet The wizards' newspaper. The paper also has an evening edition called the *Evening Prophet*.

Dark Forces, The: A Guide to Self-Protection Written by Quentin Trimble. One of the required texts for Hogwarts first-years.

Dark Lord *See* **Voldemort**.

De Mimsy-Porpington, Sir Nicholas The resident ghost of Gryffindor House; also known as Nearly Headless Nick because someone tried to behead him, but botched the job. Sir Nicholas was hit on the neck with a blunt axe forty-five times. His head is attached with just a bit of skin and he can pull it down to his shoulder by tugging on his left ear. Sir Nicholas has been dead since October 31, 1492. He wears a ruff, a doublet and hose and a plumed hat, and he is always willing to help new students find their way around Hogwarts. One of his major disappointments is not being allowed to join the Headless Hunt.

Devil's Snare A deadly plant with snakelike tendrils that wrap themselves around anyone who touches it. It likes dark, damp places and can be destroyed with fire. Devil's snare was planted by Professor Sprout to protect the pit where the philosopher's stone is hidden.

Diagon Alley A cobbled London street where witches and wizards do their shopping. Specialty shops on Diagon Alley include the Apothecary (for potion supplies), Madam Malkin's Robes for All Occasions, Eeylops Owl Emporium, Ollivanders (for wands), and Flourish and Blotts bookstore. The entrance to Diagon Alley is through a magical archway in the courtyard behind the Leaky Cauldron.

Diggle, Dedalus A wizard believed to have set off shooting stars in Kent in celebration of the banishment of Voldemort. Harry meets Diggle on his first visit to the Leaky Cauldron and remembers him as the tiny man in the violet top hat who once bowed to him while he was out shopping with the Dursleys.

Disarming Spell A spell used to disarm a wizard by ejecting his wand from his possession. The magic word for the disarming spell is *expelliarmus*.

Dragon A fantastic, fierce, fire-breathing winged creature that hatches from an egg. Dragons grow very quickly and cannot be tamed. Their eyes are their weakest

point. Albus Dumbledore is famous for discovering the twelve uses of dragon's blood.

Since owning a dragon can attract unwanted attention from muggle neighbours, dragon breeding was outlawed by the Warlocks' Convention of 1709. There are still two wild species in Britain—the common Welsh green and the Hebridean black. The Ministry of Magic keeps tabs on muggle sightings of wild dragons and uses spells to make muggles who have seen dragons forget what they have seen. *See* **Norbert**.

Draught of Living Death A powerful sleeping potion made from the powdered root of asphodel and an infusion of wormwood.

Drooble's Best Blowing Gum Magic bubble gum that makes blue bubbles which last for several days.

Dumbledore, Albus Headmaster of Hogwarts (Order of Merlin, First Class, Grand Sorcerer, Chief Warlock, Supreme Mugwump, International Confederation of Wizards). Dumbledore is a tall, thin, very old wizard whose silver hair and beard are both long enough to

tuck into his belt. He has a very long, crooked nose that seems to have been broken at least twice. He has bright, sparkling, light-blue eyes and wears half-moon spectacles. A scar above his left knee shows a perfect map of the London subway system.

Dumbledore wears high-heeled, buckled boots, long robes, and a purple cloak which sweeps the ground. He carries a put-outer to control streetlights and wears a strange, twelve-handed gold watch that has little planets moving around the edge instead of numbers. He enjoys chamber music and tenpin bowling, and is fond of muggle sweets called sherbet lemons.

Dumbledore's office at Hogwarts is a beautiful circular room filled with curious instruments and portraits of old headmasters and headmistresses. Dumbledore's phoenix, the faithful Fawkes, has a special golden perch behind the door.

Dumbledore is particularly famous for his 1945 defeat of the dark wizard Grindelwald and for his discoveries about dragon's blood. He is also known for the work he and his partner, Nicolas Flamel, did in the field of

alchemy. Many consider him to be the greates wizard of modern times.

Dursley, Aunt Marge Vernon Dursley's muggle sister an Dudley's aunt. She stays in the Dursleys' guest roor when she comes to visit. Aunt Marge hates Harry a much as her brother does.

Dursley, Dudley Harry's cousin. Dudley's doting parents Petunia and Vernon, think he is the finest boy anywhere Their pet names for him include "Duddy," "popkin, "sweetums," "Dinky Duddydums," and "Ickl Dudleykins." When Dudley was a baby, he looked lik a large, pink beach ball. He has grown into a porky pink-faced, fat-headed boy with small, watery blu eyes and smooth, blond hair. His mother thinks h looks like an angel. Harry thinks he looks like a pig i a wig. Sadly for Dudley, he comes close to turning int a pig in his first encounter with Hagrid.

Dudley hates exercise unless it involves punchin someone. One of his favourite pastimes is "Harr hunting" with his big, stupid friends, Piers Polkis Dennis, Malcolm and Gordon. Dudley and hi

friends start at Smeltings Secondary School the year Harry starts at Hogwarts. Smeltings is Uncle Vernon's old school.

Dudley and his parents are all muggles. They are ashamed of having a wizard in the family and they all hate Harry. *See* **Dursley, Vernon** *and* **Smeltings Secondary School**.

Dursley, Petunia   Dudley's mother and wife of Vernon. Petunia Dursley is Harry's muggle aunt on his mother's side; Lily Potter was her sister. Petunia is a thin, bony, horse-faced blonde with an unusually long neck that comes in handy for spying on her neighbours.

Dursley, Vernon   Dudley's muggle father; married to Harry's Aunt Petunia. Vernon Dursley is a big, beefy, purple-faced fellow with a very large black moustache and hardly any neck. Vernon works as a director at Grunnings, a local drill-manufacturing firm. His office is on the ninth floor and he always works with his back to the window.

Vernon Dursley makes the mistake of insulting Albus Dumbledore in front of Hagrid. The result is that

Hagrid tries to turn Dudley into a pig. The spell doesn't work as planned, but Dudley ends up with a pig's tail that has to be surgically removed before school starts in September.

Eeylops Owl Emporium The place to shop for an owl. It is located in Diagon Alley and stocks tawny, screech, barn, brown and snowy owls.

Elixir of Life *See* **Philosopher's stone**.

Errol The Weasley family's elderly, feeble, grey owl.

Fang Hagrid's huge black boarhound. Fang is far less ferocious than he looks.

Fantastic Beasts and Where to Find Them Written by Newt Scamander. One of the required texts for Hogwarts first-years.

Fat Friar One of Hogwarts' resident ghosts. The friar is a former student of Hufflepuff House.

Fat Lady A very fat woman in a pink silk dress whose portrait guards the entrance to Gryffindor House. *See* **Gryffindor**.

Figg, Mrs. A mad old woman who lives two streets away from the Dursleys' house. Harry is sent to stay with Mrs. Figg when the Dursleys take Dudley on his annual birthday excursion. Harry hates it because Mrs. Figg's house reeks of cabbage and she makes him look at photos of all the cats she ever owned—Tibbles, Snowy, Mr. Paws and Tufty. The summer Harry turns eleven, Mrs. Figg trips over a cat and breaks her leg. That means she can't babysit. It also means she loses some of her fondness for cats. The next time Harry stays with her, she even lets him watch television and feeds him stale chocolate cake.

Filch, Argus Hogwarts' bulgy-eyed, ill-tempered caretaker. Filch is reputed to know Hogwarts' secret passageways better than anyone. He and his cat, Mrs. Norris, patrol the hallways and try to catch students who are breaking the rules. Filch has a list of over four hundred forbidden objects posted outside his office door. He is not a proper wizard, but he is trying to learn magic by correspondence.

Finch-Fletchley, Justin One of Harry's first-year classmates. Justin belongs to Hufflepuff House.

Finnigan, Seamus A sandy-haired first-year student who i assigned to Gryffindor. Seamus' mother is a witch, bu she didn't tell her muggle husband (Seamus' dad) unt after they were married. Seamus lets Harry borro his chessmen.

Firenze A young centaur with white-blond hair, a palomin body, and pale, sapphire-blue eyes. Firenze lives in th Forbidden Forest. He comes upon Harry and Voldemor and to the irritation of his fellow centaurs, offers t carry Harry to safety on his back.

Flamel, Nicolas Dumbledore's opera-loving alchem partner and the only known maker of a philosopher stone. Flamel also owns the only stone currently i existence. The trading cards found in Chocolat Frogs record that Flamel was a six hundred an sixty-five years old last year, and that he lives i Devon with his six-hundred-and-fifty-eight-year-ol wife, Perenelle.

Flamel, Perenelle Wife of the noted alchemist Nicola Flamel, maker of the philosopher's stone. At six hundre and fifty-eight, Perenelle is seven years younger tha her husband.

Flint, Marcus Captain of Slytherin's quidditch team. Flint plays the position of chaser.

Flitwick, Professor Hogwarts' Charms teacher. Professor Flitwick is so tiny that he has to stand on a pile of books to see over his desk. When he first sees Harry Potter's name on his class register, he squeaks excitedly and topples out of sight.

Flourish and Blotts The wizard bookstore located in Diagon Alley. This is where Hogwarts students buy their school texts. The bookstore shelves are stacked from floor to ceiling with volumes ranging from postage-stamp- to paving-stone-sized.

Fluffy A monstrous, drooling, three-headed dog that guards the entrance to the pit where the philosopher's stone is hidden at Hogwarts. Fluffy belongs to Hagrid, who has loaned him to Dumbledore to protect the stone. He can only be subdued with music, which puts all of his heads to sleep.

Forbidden Forest A forest on the grounds of Hogwarts. It is off limits to students because it is full of dangerous beasts.

Fudge, Cornelius Head of the Ministry of Magic. Fudge is a portly little man who likes to wear pinstriped suits, coats or cloaks; a scarlet tie; a lime-green bowler hat and pointed purple boots. He relies heavily on Albus Dumbledore's advice and sends him owls every morning.

Galleon A gold coin used as wizard money. There are seventeen silver sickles or four hundred and ninety-three bronze knuts to a gold galleon.

Goblin A small, swarthy creature with a clever face, pointed beard, and very long fingers and feet. Goblins are a head shorter than a small eleven-year-old. They run Gringotts, the wizards' bank, and are not to be messed with. Goblins speak the language Gobbledegook.

Godric's Hollow Where Harry lived with his parents, Lily and James Potter, until they were killed by Voldemort.

Golden Snitch The most important of the three types of balls used in quidditch. The tiny, bright-gold snitch has fluttering silver wings. It is only the size of a walnut and therefore very hard to see and catch. When the seeker succeeds in catching the snitch, the team earns one hundred and fifty points and the match ends.

Goshawk, Miranda Author of *The Standard Book of Spells*, one of the required texts for Hogwarts first-years.

Goyle, Gregory A first-year student who is assigned to Slytherin. Goyle is one of Draco Malfoy's thickset, mean-looking, brutish friends.

Granger, Hermione A first-year student who is assigned to Gryffindor. Hermione is best friends with Harry Potter and Ron Weasley. She is an excellent student even though her parents (both dentists) are muggles. Hermione has bushy brown hair, a bossy voice, and rather large front teeth. Her name is pronounced Her-MY-oh-nee.

Great Hall A huge, grand room where Hogwarts school ceremonies and assemblies are held. Students sit at four long tables lit by thousands of candles that float in mid-air. Teachers sit at another long table at the top of the hall. Sumptuous feasts magically appear on golden plates. The ceiling is bewitched to look like the sky, and at night, its velvety blackness is dotted with stars.

Gringotts The wizards' goblin-run bank, which is heavily protected by spells and enchantments. Next to Hogwarts,

Gringotts is the safest place in the world. It is rumoured that dragons guard its high-security vaults, which are located hundreds of miles beneath the London subway system. Aboveground, Gringotts is a snowy-white building which towers above the shops in Diagon Alley. A goblin garbed in scarlet and gold stands guard at its burnished bronze doors. Inside, engraved silver doors open onto a vast, marble hall where a hundred goblins sit on high stools behind a very long counter—weighing coins, examining jewels, or scribbling away in ledgers. Goblin guides escort customers along narrow, twisting, underground passages to their vaults, which are reached by small railway carts that seem to know their own way.

Griphook The goblin who escorts Harry and Hagrid to the Potters' vault on Harry's first visit to Gringotts.

Grunnings The drill-manufacturing company where Vernon Dursley is a director. Dursley's office is on the ninth floor.

Gryffindor, Godric One of the four founders of Hogwarts. *See* **Hogwarts School of Witchcraft and Wizardry**.

Gryffindor One of the four Hogwarts houses; established by Godric Gryffindor, who valued bravery above all other virtues. Albus Dumbledore was once a member of this house. The year Harry Potter starts at Hogwarts, the sorting hat selects Harry, Ron Weasley, Hermione Granger, Neville Longbottom, Seamus Finnigan, Dean Thomas, Parvinder Patil and Lavender Brown for Gryffindor.

Gryffindor's colours are scarlet and gold and its emblem is a gold lion on a scarlet ground. Professor McGonagall is the head of the house. Sir Nicholas de Mimsy-Porpington is the resident ghost. The entrance to Gryffindor House is covered by a portrait of the Fat Lady, who needs to hear the secret password before her portrait swings open to uncover a round hole in the wall. The hole opens onto Gryffindor's round, common room. Boys' and girls' dormitories are located in a tower on top of a spiral staircase. Harry's room holds five four-poster beds hung with curtains of deep-red velvet. *See* **Fat Lady**.

Hagrid, Rubeus Keeper of Keys and Grounds at Hogwarts. Hagrid is a soft-hearted giant of a man—twice as tall

and five times as wide as a normal person. His hands are the size of dustbin lids and his feet, the size of baby dolphins. He is a muscular, wild-looking fellow with beetle-black eyes, shaggy black hair, and a beard that hides most of his face. He is a notoriously bad cook and his trademark is an oversize black moleskin coat.

Hagrid is especially fond of large, rather dangerous animals. He has a pet boarhound named Fang and a three-headed dog he calls Fluffy. He once tried to raise a giant spider named Aragog and a Norwegian ridgeback dragon named Norbert.

Hagrid lives in a cottage at the edge of the Forbidden Forest. He is a former Hogwarts student who was expelled in his third year for a crime he did not commit. His wand was broken as a result, and he is not supposed to do any magic. Nevertheless, he has the trust of Dumbledore, even though his pink umbrella sometimes causes strange phenomena (like Dudley Dursley's curly pig's tail) that he asks his friends not to mention.

Hagrid is especially fond of Harry. When Harry's parents are killed, it is Hagrid who delivers the one-year-old orphan to the Dursleys' on a flying motorcycle borrowed from Sirius Black. Hagrid is also the one who finally delivers Harry's invitation to attend Hogwarts. He buys Harry his first real birthday present (his snowy owl Hedwig) and presents him with an album of photographs of his parents.

He-Who-Must-Not-Be-Named *See* **Voldemort**.

Hebridean Black A wild dragon native to Britain.

Hedwig Harry's snowy owl. She was a gift from Hagrid on Harry's eleventh birthday. Harry found her name in *A History of Magic*. He uses her to send messages.

Higgs, Terence The seeker on Slytherin's quidditch team.

History of Magic, A Written by Bathilda Bagshot. One of the required texts for Hogwarts first-years.

Hog's Head The village pub where Hagrid wins his dragon in a game of cards.

Hogwarts Express The scarlet steam engine that transports students to and from Hogwarts each term. The train

leaves from platform nine and three-quarters a London's King's Cross station at precisely 11 o'cloc every September 1.

Hogwarts School of Witchcraft and Wizardry One of th finest schools of wizardry in the world, Hogwarts i situated atop a high mountain on the shore of a grea black lake inhabited by a giant squid. The forest on th grounds is full of dangerous beasts and is forbidde territory to all pupils.

Hogwarts was founded over a thousand years ago b Godric Gryffindor, Helga Hufflepuff, Rowena Ravencla and Salazar Slytherin—the four greatest wizards an witches of their age. Together, they built a huge, magica turreted castle with enormous meeting rooms, hall mazes, secret rooms, temperamental doors (some o which need to be tickled before they open), and a hundre and forty-two staircases—including some with vanishin steps. Each of the founders established a house an chose students who exemplified the virtues they value most. Gryffindor prized bravery, nerve and chivalr Hufflepuff, loyalty, integrity and hard work Ravenclaw, wit and learning; and Slytherin, cunnin

and ambition. While the founders were alive, they selected worthy students for each of their houses. Gryffindor enchanted his own hat—which became the sorting hat—so that it could make the selections once he and his fellow founders were dead and gone. By Harry Potter's time, the sorting hat chooses the house to which new students will belong.

Each Hogwarts house has its own symbol and its own colours. Students' triumphs earn points for their respective houses, while students who misbehave and break rules lose house points. The competition between houses is quite intense because, at the end of the year, the house with the most points is awarded the coveted house cup.

The Hogwarts school song is sung to each student's favourite tune, so everyone finishes at a different time. Official school correspondence is written in emerald-green ink and sealed with purple wax bearing the school's coat of arms. The school term begins on September 1. It takes seven years to complete the Hogwarts course of studies.

Hogwarts castle is protected by a variety of enchantments and it is considered one of the safest places on earth. Its location is invisible to muggles, who see only old ruins and signs warning people to keep out.

Hooch, Madam Hogwarts' teacher of broom-flying. Madam has short, grey hair and yellow, hawk-like eyes.

Hufflepuff, Helga One of the four founders of Hogwarts. *See* **Hogwarts School of Witchcraft and Wizardry**.

Hufflepuff One of the four Hogwarts houses; established by Helga Hufflepuff, who valued loyalty and hard work above all other virtues. Hufflepuff's colours are black and yellow and its emblem is a black badger on a yellow ground.

Hut-on-the-Rock, The Sea A shabby, isolated hut where the Dursleys retreat in a desperate attempt to escape the bombardment of letters Harry is getting from Hogwarts. No matter what the Dursleys do, though, the letters seem to find Harry. The first letter is addressed to Harry in his cupboard under the stairs. When Uncle Vernon destroys it, dozens more follow.

addressed to Harry in the smallest bedroom. They come in through the windows, under the doors, and even down the fireplace. When the Dursleys arrive at the Railview Hotel after driving all day, a hundred letters are waiting for Harry. Harry's letter is finally delivered to him in person when the Dursleys are at the Hut-on-the-Rock.

nvisibility Cloak   A magical cloak that makes its wearer invisible.

igger, Arsenius   Author of *Magical Drafts and Potions*, one of the required texts for Hogwarts first-years.

ohnson, Angelina   One of the chasers on Gryffindor's quidditch team.

ordan, Lee   A Gryffindor boy who sometimes serves as the commentator for quidditch games. Lee is a good friend of the Weasley twins.

eeper   A quidditch position. The keeper tries to stop the other team's chasers from getting the quaffle ball through the hoops in a quidditch match.

Knut A small bronze coin used as wizard money. There ar
twenty-nine bronze knuts to a silver sickle.

Leaky Cauldron A tiny, inconspicuous, grubby-lookin
London pub which is invisible to muggles. The pu
serves as the entrance to Diagon Alley, where man
wizard shops are found. Access is through a magica
archway which appears when a particular brick in th
wall of the rear courtyard is tapped three times. Th
special brick is three up and two across from the dustbi
When the brick is tapped, it quivers and wriggles until
hole appears and grows into a large archway that open
onto Diagon Alley. Once travellers step through, th
hole disappears. On his first trip to the Leaky Cauldro
with Hagrid, Harry meets many witches and wizards–
including the bald, old barman Tom—who are delighte
to make his acquaintance.

Leg-locker Curse A curse which uses the magic word
locomotor mortis to lock its victim's legs togethe
Draco Malfoy uses the leg-locker curse on poor Nevil
Longbottom, who has to bunnyhop all the way hom
from the Hogwarts library.

Liquorice Wand A type of wizard candy.

Little Whinging The Surrey community where the Dursleys live.

Locomotor Mortis The magic words used for the leg-locker curse.

Longbottom, Neville A first-year student who is assigned to Gryffindor. Round-faced, accident-prone, forgetful Neville lives with his grandmother, who is delighted when he finally shows some aptitude for wizardry at the age of eight. It happens when his Great Uncle Algie drops him out of an upstairs window by mistake. To everyone's delight, Neville bounces! Uncle Algie is so pleased that he buys him a toad, Trevor. Neville's grandmother gives him a remembrall to help him remember things, but Neville is still forgetful and not very good at Charms or Potions. Herbology is his best subject.

MacDougal, Morag A first-year student at Hogwarts.

Madam Malkin's Robes for All Occasions The robe-maker's shop in Diagon Alley. The proprietor is a squat, smiling

witch robed in mauve. Harry first meets Draco Malfo[y] at Madam Malkin's.

Magical Drafts and Potions Written by Arsenius Jigge[r.] One of the required texts for Hogwarts first-years.

Magical Theory Written by Adalbert Waffling. One of th[e] required texts for Hogwarts first-years.

Malfoy, Draco A first-year student who is assigned t[o] Slytherin. Malfoy is a conceited, sneaky bully who[m] Harry hates even more than his porky cousin Dudle[y.] He has a pale, pointed face and is rarely seen withou[t] his brutish sidekicks, Crabbe and Goyle.

McGonagall, Minerva Professor, deputy headmistress, an[d] head of Gryffindor House. McGonagall is a ta[ll] severe-looking woman who favours emerald-gree[n] robes and cloaks. She wears square eyeglasses and pul[ls] her black hair back into a tight bun. Strict and cleve[r,] McGonagall is definitely not a teacher to cross. Sh[e] teaches transfiguration and can change shape at wi[ll.] She has often disguised herself as a cat. McGonaga[ll] arranges for Harry to join the Gryffindor quiddit[c]

team even though he is only a first-year student. She also gives Harry his first flying-broom, a Nimbus Two Thousand which is delivered by six large screech owls.

Ministry of Magic A multi-department agency headed by Cornelius Fudge. One of the ministry's roles is keeping muggles unaware that there are witches and wizards everywhere. The ministry also regulates underage wizards, experimental charms, magical creatures, international relations, magical games and sport, and the improper use of magic.

Mirror of Erised An enchanted mirror that shows only the deepest, most desperate desires of the person gazing into it. The mirror stands as high as the ceiling. It is encased in an ornate gold frame carved with the inscription "*Erised stra ehru oyt ube cafru oyt on wohsi.*"

Monkshood *See* **Wolfsbane**.

Mountain Troll *See* **Troll**.

Muggle A non-magic person.

Nearly Headless Nick *See* **De Mimsy-Porpington, Sir Nicholas**.

Nimbus Two Thousand The best and fastest
flying-broom made.

Norbert Hagrid's illegal pet dragon. Norbert is a rar
Norwegian ridgeback which hatches from a huge, black
egg that Hagrid wins in a card game at the Hog's Head
pub. The hatchling has a long snout, bulging orange
eyes, and huge spiny wings on a skinny black body. I
has a ravenous appetite and feeds on a bucket o
brandy and chicken blood every half hour. In a week'
time, it triples in size and graduates to solid foods–
dead rats by the crateful. Hagrid finally concedes tha
he can't keep his dragon. (It's not safe to have a fire
breathing creature in a wooden house.) Harry, Ron an
Hermione arrange to have Norbert sent to Charli
Weasley, who studies dragons in Romania. *See* **Drago**

Norris, Mrs. Mr. Filch's scrawny, bulgy-eyed, dus
coloured cat. She patrols the halls of Hogwarts an
reports to Filch if she sees anyone misbehaving
Hogwarts students are not too fond of Mrs. Norris

Norwegian ridgeback A rare, black dragon species.

Number Four, Privet Drive The Dursleys' house in Litt
Whinging, Surrey (in southeast England).

Ollivanders A wand shop located in Diagon Alley. The Ollivanders have been makers of fine wands since 382 BC. "The wand chooses the wizard," according to Mr. Ollivander, and no two Ollivander wands are quite the same. Each has a core made from a powerful magical substance. The core of Voldemort's thirteen-and-a-half-inch yew wand is a phoenix feather. Harry's eleven-inch holly wand contains a feather from the same phoenix. These two feathers are the only ones this particular phoenix has ever given.

One Thousand Magical Herbs and Fungi Written by Phyllida Spore. One of the required texts for Hogwarts first-years.

Owl Post The wizards' "airmail" messenger service.

Parkinson, Pansy A hard-faced girl who belongs to Slytherin House.

Patil, Parvati A first-year student who is assigned to Gryffindor. Parvati's twin sister, Padma, is also a Hogwarts student. Parvati and Lavender Brown are good friends.

Peeves A nasty little poltergeist with dark, wicked eyes an
a wide mouth. Peeves wears an orange bow tie and a ha
covered in bells. He delights in mischief of all sort:
from stuffing keyholes with chewing gum to throwin
water balloons at unsuspecting students. Peeve
makes life particularly difficult for first-years. He give
them wrong directions, drops and throws things ɑ
them, pulls rugs out from under their feet, an
sneaks up behind and grabs their noses. Only the
Bloody Baron can control him.

Perks, Sally-Anne A first-year student at Hogwarts.

Petrificus Totalus A body-binding curse which leaves i
victims totally rigid and immobile, except for their eye
Hermione is forced to use this curse on Nevil
Longbottom when he tries to stop his friends fror
going out and getting Gryffindor into trouble. Neville
legs snap together, his arms spring to his sides, an
even his jaws jam shut so that he can't speak.

Philosopher's Stone A legendary, blood-red stone which ca
change any metal to gold. The stone can also produc
the elixir of life, which grants immortality to anyor
who drinks it. Nicolas Flamel is the only known make

of the philosopher's stone and owns the only stone currently in existence. Also known as the sorcerer's stone.

ince, Madam Hogwarts' thin, irritable librarian, who looks a bit like a vulture.

latform Nine and Three-quarters Located at King's Cross station in London. The Hogwarts Express leaves from this platform at 11 o'clock sharp every September 1. The platform is reached by walking straight through the ticket barrier between muggle platforms nine and ten.

olkiss, Piers Dudley Dursley's nasty best friend.

omfrey, Poppy Madam Pomfrey is the Hogwarts school physician.

otter, Harry Born on July 31, Harry is the orphaned son of James and Lily Potter, who are killed by the evil Voldemort when Harry is just a year old. Voldemort tries to kill Harry too. His attempt is not successful, but it leaves Harry with a thin, lightning-bolt-shaped scar on his forehead.

When his parents are killed, Albus Dumbledore ask
Hagrid to bring Harry to live with his only relatives
Vernon and Petunia Dursley and their young so
Dudley. Petunia is a sister to Harry's mother, Lily. Th
Dudleys are muggles (non-magic folk) who despis
wizards and magic. They fear Harry and treat hir
badly. They also keep his wizardly heritage a secret
Harry does not discover his true identity until hi
eleventh birthday, when he learns how his parents reall
died and how he got his scar. He also discovers that h
is famous in the wizard world: he is the only perso
ever to have survived an attack by the wickec
powerful Voldemort.

Harry is a small, skinny boy with a thin face and rath
knobby knees. He has his father's unruly, jet-black ha
and his mother's green eyes. He wears round glasses, and h
most distinguishing feature is his lightning-bolt-shape
scar. *See also*: **Dursley, Dudley; Hagrid, Rubeu
Hut-on-the-Rock, The Sea; Ollivanders**; *and* **Voldemor

Potter, James and Lily Harry's parents, both of whom we
powerful wizards. Lily and James were killed by the ev
Voldemort on Halloween night when Harry was or

year old, but Lily managed to protect her son. Red-haired, green-eyed Lily Potter was Petunia Dursley's sister and muggle-born. James Potter was a tall, thin man with untidy black hair and glasses. The Potters lived at Godric's Hollow.

Potter, Lily *See* **Potter, James and Lily**.

Privet Drive *See* **Number 4, Privet Drive**.

Pucey, Adrian One of the chasers on Slytherin's quidditch team.

Pumpkin Pasty A pumpkin-flavoured turnover.

Put-outer A device that looks like a silver cigarette lighter. Wizards click it to snuff or light street lamps. Dumbledore uses a put-outer on Privet Drive on the night Harry Potter is brought to stay with the Dursleys.

Quaffle One of the three types of balls used in quidditch. The bright-red quaffle is about the size of a soccer ball. Ten points are earned each time a chaser manages to get the quaffle through one of the opposing team's hoops.

Quidditch This is the wizards' national sport, which is played on flying broomsticks. There are seven hundred ways to commit a quidditch foul. There are seven players on a quidditch team: three chasers, two beaters, a keeper and a seeker. A quidditch field (also called a pitch) has three fifty-foot-high golden hoops at each end. The chasers try to get the red, soccer-ball-sized quaffle through the hoops to score ten points. The keeper tries to prevent the opposing team from scoring. The keeper is assisted by two black bludger balls which rock around trying to knock players off their brooms. The beaters knock the bludgers away with small clubs that look like baseball or rounders bats. The seeker chases the tiny, silver-winged golden snitch, which is very hard to see and catch. (The record is three months.) Capturing the snitch earns one hundred and fifty points and ends the game. The game is not over until the snitch has been caught.

Quirrell, Professor Hogwarts' Defence Against the Dark Arts teacher in Harry's first year at the school. Quirrell is pale and twitchy-eyed and affects a stutter. His classroom reeks of garlic and a funny smell hangs around the large purple turban he always wears. Quirrell claims

the turban was a gift from an African prince. In reality, it hides Quirrell's master, Voldemort, for whom Quirrell tries to get the philosopher's stone.

avenclaw, Rowena One of the four founders of Hogwarts. *See* **Hogwarts School of Witchcraft and Wizardry**.

avenclaw One of the four Hogwarts houses; established by Rowena Ravenclaw, who valued wit and learning above all other virtues. Ravenclaw's colours are blue and bronze and its emblem is a bronze eagle on a blue ground.

emembrall A marble-sized glass ball which seems to be filled with white smoke. If the ball is held tightly and it turns red, it means the holder has forgotten something. Neville Longbottom's grandmother sends him a remembrall because he is always forgetting things.

onan A red-haired, chestnut-bodied centaur who lives in the Forbidden Forest.

Rowling, J.K. Joanne Kathleen (Jo) Rowling, author of the Harry Potter series. Rowling was born in Chipping Sodbury in the UK in 1965. She studied French at the University of Exeter in Devon. She later taught French in Edinburgh, where she currently lives with her daughter.

Scabbers Ron Weasley's fat, gray rat, which used to belong to his brother Percy. Ron got Scabbers when Percy received an owl as a reward for becoming a prefect.

Scamander, Newt Author of *Fantastic Beasts and Where to Find Them*, one of the required texts for Hogwarts first-years.

Seeker A quidditch position. The seeker's job is to capture the tiny, silver-winged, golden snitch. Capturing the snitch earns one hundred and fifty points and ends the game.

Sickle A silver coin used as wizard money. There are seventeen silver sickles to a gold galleon, and twenty-nine bronze knuts to a silver sickle.

lytherin, Salazar   One of the four founders of
Hogwarts and a noted parselmouth (someone
who speaks the language of snakes). Slytherin
believed that magical learning should be restricted
to all-magic families and that muggle-born students
should be excluded. His views eventually led to a
falling out with the other founders, and he left
Hogwarts. *See* **Hogwarts School of Witchcraft
and Wizardry**.

lytherin   One of the four Hogwarts houses; established
by Salazar Slytherin, who valued cunning and
ambition above all other virtues. Slytherin's
colours are green and silver and its emblem is a silver
snake on a green ground. Until Harry shows up at
Hogwarts, Slytherin has won the house cup for six
years in a row.

mallest Bedroom   Dudley Dursley's second bedroom,
where he keeps all the toys that don't fit into his first
bedroom. This is where the Dursleys move Harry
after he receives his first Hogwarts letter, which is
addressed to him in his cupboard under the stairs.

Smeltings Secondary School Vernon Dursley's alma mater, which Dudley and his friends will also attend. The Smeltings uniform consists of a maroon tailcoat, orange knickerbockers, a boater (flat straw hat) and a knobbly stick. Students train for later life by hitting each other with their sticks when the teachers aren't looking.

Snape, Severus Professor and head of Slytherin House, Snape is the Potions instructor, but he really wants to be teaching Defence Against the Dark Arts. His classes are held in a cold, creepy dungeon stocked with pickled animals floating in glass jars. Snape has greasy black hair, a hooked nose, sallow skin and cold, empty black eyes. Harry is convinced that Snape hates him. He eventually learns why. Snape attended Hogwarts with Harry Potter's father, James, whom he always resented. However, James Potter saved Snape's life when a practical joke went wrong and Snape owes him (and therefore his son) a grudging debt.

Snitch *See* **Golden Snitch**.

orcerer's Stone *See* **Philosopher's Stone**.

orting Hat A frayed, patched and very dirty pointed wizard's hat that belonged to Godric Gryffindor, one of the founders of Hogwarts. New students take part in a sorting ceremony during which the sorting hat is placed on their heads. The hat decides which Hogwarts house each student will belong to. *See* **Hogwarts School of Witchcraft and Wizardry**.

pinnet, Alicia One of the chasers on Gryffindor's quidditch team.

pore, Phyllida Author of *One Thousand Magical Herbs and Fungi*, one of the required texts for Hogwarts first-years.

prout, Professor A squat little witch with flyaway hair under a patched hat. She teaches Herbology, and usually has earth on her clothes and fingernails.

tandard Book of Spells, The Written by Miranda Goshawk. One of the required texts for Hogwarts first-years.

Stonewall High   The local high school which Harr
would have attended had he not gone to Hogwarts.

Switch, Emeric   Author of *A Beginners' Guide t
Transfiguration*, one of the required texts fc
Hogwarts first-years.

Thomas, Dean   A first-year student who is assigne
to Gryffindor.

Transfiguration   Complex, dangerous magic used t
turn one thing into something else. Professc
McGonagall teaches the Transfiguration cla
at Hogwarts.

Trevor   Neville Longbottom's pet toad. Trevor wi
gift from Neville's Great Uncle Algie.

Trimble, Quentin   Author of *The Dark Forces: A Gui
to Self-Protection*, one of the required texts f
Hogwarts first-years.

Troll   A foul-smelling, grey-skinned, twelve-foot monst
that carries a huge wooden club. Trolls have lump

boulder-like bodies; short, thick legs; long arms; and flat, horny feet. Their small, bald heads perch on their shoulders like coconuts. Their distinctive smell is a like mixture of old socks and filthy toilets.

Unicorn A rare, pure creature whose horns and tail-hair are used in wizards' wands and potions. The unicorn's silver blood has the power to restore life even to someone who is an inch from death, although the price is a terrible one. Slaying something pure and defenceless to save yourself is a monstrous crime, and the perpetrator is cursed from the moment the unicorn's blood touches his lips.

Unicorn foals are pure gold. They turn silver at the age of two, and pure white when they are full-grown, at about the age of seven. They begin to grow horns when they are about four.

Vault Seven Hundred and Thirteen Hogwarts' top-security vault at Gringotts. Unlike Gringotts' regular vaults, seven hundred and thirteen has no keyhole. The door melts away when a goblin strokes it with a finger, but anyone else who tried this would be

sucked through and trapped for at least ten year. Dumbledore sends Hagrid to collect a grubby littl brown package that is stored in the vault. Late that day, July 31, the vault is broken into. Dar wizards or witches are suspected.

Viridian, Vindictus Author of *Curses and Counter-Curses*.

Voldemort A powerful wizard who goes bad an terrorizes the wizard world, killing all who oppos him and recruiting followers to the dark side. Mo wizards fear him so much that they never refer him by name, but rather, as You-Know-Who He-Who-Must-Not-Be-Named or the dark lor Albus Dumbledore is the only wizard Voldemo fears and one of the few who dare to speak his name

Voldemort kills Harry's parents, James and Li Potter, and tries to kill the one-year-old Harry well. His murderous green blast leaves Harry wi his lightning-shaped scar, but bounces back Voldemort, turning him into mere shadow ar vapour. For many years after the attac Voldemort can only take on human form when

shares another body. He needs unicorn's blood and the philosopher's stone to regain his former power. *See* **Ollivanders**; **Philosopher's Stone**; **Quirrell, Professor**; *and* **Unicorn**.

Waffling, Adalbert Author of *Magical Theory*, one of the required texts for Hogwarts first-years.

Weasley, Arthur and Molly Ron's parents. Ron's mother, Molly, is a short, plump, kindly woman who conjures wonderful meals and often carries a large clothes brush in her bag. Mrs. Weasley sends Harry and her children homemade sweets and hand-knitted sweaters (jumpers) each Christmas. Ron's sweater is always maroon, which he hates. Arthur Weasley is a thin, balding man who wears glasses. All seven of his children have inherited his red hair. Arthur heads the Misuse of Muggle Artifacts Office at the Ministry of Magic and is fascinated by muggles and muggle affairs. The Weasleys don't have much money. They live outside a village called Ottery St. Catchpole in a house called The Burrow. Their ancient owl, Errol, delivers their messages.

Weasley, Bill The oldest of Ron's red-headed brothers, Bill used to be the Gryffindor head boy. He is now in Egypt, working as a curse-breaker for Gringotts (the wizards' bank). Bill is tall and wears his long hair tied back in a ponytail. He is a fashionable dresser who sports a fang earring and dragonhide boots.

Weasley, Charlie The second-oldest of Ron's red-headed brothers and an alumnus of Hogwarts. Charlie was captain of Gryffindor's quidditch team. Stockily built like his twin brothers, good-natured Charlie has a very freckled and weather-beaten broad face. He is now studying dragons in Romania.

Weasley, Fred and George Ron's older brothers, who are identical, red-headed twins. Although the twins are always getting into trouble and constantly scheming up new tricks, they both get really good grades. Fred and George are beaters on Gryffindor's quidditch team. They are shorter and stockier than their brothers Percy and Ron.

Weasley, George *See* **Weasley, Fred and George**.

Weasley, Ginny The youngest member of the Weasley family and the only girl. Like all of her siblings, Ginny has red hair. She has a crush on Harry Potter.

Weasley, Molly *See* **Weasley, Arthur and Molly**.

Weasley, Percy One of Ron's red-headed older brothers. Tall, lanky Percy is a prefect at Hogwarts, and he wears his shiny, silver prefect's badge everywhere he goes. He is older than the twins and is always fussing about school rules and regulations. Like all the other Weasleys, Percy belongs to Gryffindor House.

Weasley, Ron Harry's best friend. Ron is the sixth child in his family to attend Hogwarts, and like his siblings, he belongs to Gryffindor House. Ron is a tall, thin, gangly, freckle-faced redhead with big hands and feet and a long nose. He never gets anything new, but has to make do with hand-me-downs from his older brothers. Even his pet rat, Scabbers, used to belong to his brother Percy. Ron gets Scabbers when Percy gets an owl (Hermes) to acknowledge his appointment as a Hogwarts prefect. Ron is an avid quidditch fan and every inch of his bedroom at

home is covered with posters of his favourite team
the Chudley Cannons. His favourite comic book
are *The Adventures of Martin Miggs, The Ma*
Muggle. When Ron was three, he broke his brothe
Fred's toy broomstick. Fred retaliated by turnin
Ron's teddy bear into a spider. Ron hasn't muc
liked spiders since.

Wingardium Leviosa The charm that makes objects fly.

Wolfsbane A herb that is also known as monkshoc
or aconite.

Wood, Oliver Captain and keeper for the Gryffindc
quidditch team. Oliver is a burly youth who is fou
years ahead of Harry at Hogwarts.

Wormwood A plant which can be infused (steeped
liquid) and mixed with powdered asphodel root
make the powerful sleeping potion known as t
draught of living death.

You-Know-Who *See* **Voldemort**.

Zabini, Blaise A first-year student who is assigned
to Slytherin.

Autographs & Notes:

Autographs & Notes:

Autographs & Notes:

Autographs & Notes:

Autographs & Notes:

Autographs & Notes: